THE Kid's GUIDE TO GOOD GRAMMAR

THE Kid's GUIDE TO GOOD GRAMMAR

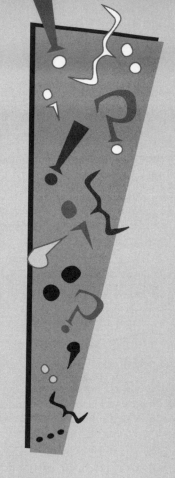

What You Need to Know About **Punctuation**, **Sentence Structure**, **Spelling**, and More

By Dorothy McKerns, M.Ed., Ph.D., CCC-SLP
and Leslie Motchkavitz

Illustrated by Anna Dewdney

LOWELL HOUSE JUVENILE
LOS ANGELES
NTC/Contemporary Publishing Group

Library of Congress Cataloging-in-Publication Data

McKerns, Dorothy
   The kid's guide to good grammar / by Dorothy McKerns and Leslie
Motchkavitz.
     p. cm.
   Summary: Presents the fundamental rules of grammar, covering
sentence structure, parts of speech, common errors, and more.
   ISBN 1-56565-697-0 (pbk. : alk. paper)
   1. English language--Grammar--Juvenile literature. [1. English
language--Grammar.] I. Motchkavitz, Leslie McKerns. II. Title.
PE1112.M39 1998
428.2--dc21

                                                98-20827
                                                    CIP
                                                       AC

Published by Lowell House
A division of NTC/Contemporary Publishing Group, Inc.
4255 West Touhy Avenue, Lincolnwood (Chicago), Illinois 60646-1975 U.S.A.

Requests for such permissions should be addressed to:
NTC/Contemporary Publishing Group, Inc.
4255 West Touhy Avenue, Lincolnwood (Chicago), Illinois 60646-1975 U.S.A.

Managing Director and Publisher: Jack Artenstein
Director of Publishing Services: Rena Copperman
Editorial Director, Juvenile: Brenda Pope-Ostrow
Director of Juvenile Development: Amy Downing
Typesetting and Design: Carolyn Wendt

Lowell House books can be purchased at special discounts
when ordered in bulk for premiums and special sales.
Contact Customer Service at the above address,
or call 1-800-323-4900.

Printed and bound in the United States of America
10 9 8 7 6 5 4 3 2 1

CONTENTS

Do you have a reluctant grammar student? *The Kid's Guide to Good Grammar* is an easy-to-use handbook for youngsters, whether they love grammar or have difficulty mastering the basics. This book includes:

○ Practice Makes Perfect! sections, which offer games, crafts, and other activities to reinforce important grammar concepts. These activities can easily be adapted for classroom use.

○ Rules to Remember sidebars, which draw young readers' attention to rules they should memorize.

○ Loads of charts and word lists, such as the Irregular Verb Chart and 240 Common Spelling Words, for students to use as a helpful reference.

○ Excerpts from favorite classics, so that while they are learning grammar, readers are also being introduced to classic novels by authors Mark Twain, Frances Hodgson Burnett, Lewis Carroll, and Jack London.

For easy reference, following you'll find the Practice Makes Perfect! activities listed by subject:

On the Parts of Speech: The Most and Least Game, page 42

INTRODUCTION

What if there were no sentences? No language? What would happen to watching television, reading a book, or going out to dinner? You couldn't tell your waiter what you wanted, because you couldn't put your words together in an understandable way, and with no written menus, how would you know what the restaurant serves anyway? Breathe a sigh of relief because there are sentences in this world. They are our key to communicating.

So, in order to communicate, you need to learn how sentences work. And for that, you need grammar. That's what *The Kid's Guide to Good Grammar* is all about, and it's no ordinary grammar book.

You'll be treated to excerpts from some favorite stories. You'll join Alice, in *Alice in Wonderland* and *Through the Looking Glass* by Lewis Carroll, on her zany run-ins with some pretty funny characters. You'll also meet the kids from *The Secret Garden* by Frances Hodgson Burnett and discover with them the wonder of a special and magical place. You'll follow Tom Sawyer's escapades in *The Adventures of Tom Sawyer* by Mark Twain. *The Call of the Wild* by Jack London may be the closest you'll ever get to riding a dogsled through snowy mountain trails in the Yukon in search of gold!

What's more, you'll find loads of games, puzzles, and arts and crafts projects to keep you dazzled. The best part is that

Alice in Wonderland

The Secret Garden

The Adventures of Tom Sawyer

The Call of the Wild

while you are having so much fun, you will learn how to use the English language more effectively to become a better communicator.

CHAPTER 1 | PARTS OF SPEECH

Quick! Can you name the eight parts of speech? Here goes: nouns, pronouns, verbs, adverbs, adjectives, conjunctions, prepositions, and interjections. But surprise! These eight building blocks of sentences have lots of secrets. Did you know that sometimes you can't see a noun? Or that verbs don't always mean "action"? Once you become familiar with how the eight parts of speech operate, you'll be able to use them to create great grammatical sentences.

RECOGNIZING NOUNS

A noun names or labels a person, place, or thing. Often, nouns are things you can see and touch. Look around you, and make a list of all the objects you see. If you're in the kitchen, you might list *cup, table, chair, toaster, sink, floor, cupboard,* and *telephone.*

Some nouns—such as *peace, beauty, happiness,* and *strength*—stand for ideas.

Other nouns represent sounds, smells, or feelings: *crash, bang, whistle, groan, echo, scent, stink, terror, pain, grief, awe,* and *delight.* Can you tell which signify sounds, smells, or feelings?

Many kinds of nouns run through this selection below. Can you find them?

The Adventures of Tom Sawyer

At last Tom rose slowly and softly, and started alone. But the first step he made wrung such a hideous creak from the crazy floor that he sank down almost dead with fright. He never made a second attempt. The boys lay there counting the

dragging moments till it seemed to them that time must be done and eternity growing gray; and then they were grateful to note that at last the sun was setting.

HINT ON HUNTING NOUNS: Ask yourself these questions: Is it a person? Is it a place? Is it an object that can be seen or touched? Is it a feeling? Is it an idea? Two nouns in this selection are measurements of time. Can you find them? One means "a little bit of time," and the other means "forever."

● ●

Practice Makes Perfect!

COOL COLLECTIBLE CAPS

Collect your favorite pictures of nouns and make some cool pins or picture frames!

WHAT YOU NEED: metal bottle caps, small hammer, decoupage glue, paintbrush, scissors, small photos or magazine pictures, small safety pins, inexpensive picture frames (any size), craft glue.

WHAT YOU DO:
Find pictures of nouns that fit into categories: jungle animals, tropical plants, toys, rock stars . . . the list is endless! **Cut your pictures** to fit into the bottle caps. If you are decorating

picture frames, you'll want twelve to fifteen caps. To make jewelry pins, you only need one cap per pin. **Press the pictures** into the caps. **Tap the edges** of the cap all the way around so that they are crimped in and hold the picture in place. With the paintbrush, **cover**

the picture with a thin coat of decoupage glue (this will protect it). For picture frames, **glue the caps** around the frame. For pins, **glue a small safety pin** to the back of each cap. (Make sure you don't glue the part of the safety pin that opens and closes.)

PROPER NOUNS

A proper noun is the specific name of a person, place, or thing. Take a look at this excerpt below. Can you pick out the examples of proper nouns?

The Secret Garden

Mary made the long voyage to England under the care of an officer's wife, who was taking her children to leave them in a boarding-school. She was very much absorbed in her own little boy and girl, and was rather glad to hand the child over to the woman Mr. Archibald Craven sent to meet her, in London. The woman was his housekeeper at Misselthwaite Manor, and her name was Mrs. Medlock.

HINT ON HUNTING PROPER NOUNS: All the proper names have capital letters. You should find the names of three different people and of three different places. Did you?

You are right if you found these people: Mary, Mr. Archibald Craven, and Mrs. Medlock. These are the places: England, London, Misselthwaite Manor.

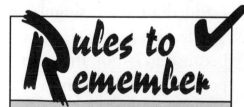

Rules to Remember ✔

You must use a capital letter for proper nouns.

11

SINGULARS AND PLURALS

Nouns are singular when there is one and plural if there are more than one. Can you find five plural nouns in this excerpt?

The Secret Garden

If she had been friends with Colin she would have run to show him her presents at once, and they would have looked at the pictures and read some of the gardening books and perhaps tried playing the games, and he would have enjoyed himself so much . . .

HINT ON HUNTING PLURALS:

The plural nouns have the letter *s* added to their singular form. Watch out! *Perhaps* is not a noun because it is not the name of a person, place, or thing.

POSSESSIVE NOUNS

Possessive nouns are nouns that show ownership or belonging.

Rules to Remember

To turn a singular noun into a plural, you usually add an *s*. However, keep in mind these few exceptions:

For words that end with a consonant followed by *y*, change the *y* to *i* and then add *es*: *ruby* → *rubies*; *duty* → *duties*.

For words that end with *ss*, *sh*, *ch*, or *x*, add *es*: *glass* → *glasses*; *wish* → *wishes*; *watch* → *watches*; *box* → *boxes*. Notice that when you say the plurals of these words, the *es* makes a new syllable.

For words that end with *f*, change the *f* to *v* and add *es*: *calf* → *calves*; *half* → *halves*.

Some words become different words entirely when they are made plural: *mouse* → *mice*; *foot* → *feet*.

A few words are the same plural as they are singular, for example: *deer*; *fish*.

Possessive nouns always contain an apostrophe, which looks like a floating comma. A possessive noun can be formed in the following ways:

1. Add apostrophe *s* (*'s*) to a singular noun such as *boy* to make *boy's*.
2. Add an apostrophe after the *s* to plurals that already end with *s* or *es,* such as *girls* to make *girls'* or *foxes* to make *foxes',* and to names that end with *s,* such as *Charles,* to make *Charles'.*
3. Put an apostrophe *s* on plurals that do not end with *s* or *es,* such as *men* to *men's.*

The Adventures of Tom Sawyer

. . . When he comes to the right girl, he'll know it, without any telling. Girls' faces always tell on them.
Every time he stole a glance at the girls' side of the room Becky's face troubled him.

Which possessive noun is singular, and which is plural? If you picked *girls'* as the plural, you are right. *Becky's* is the singular possessive noun, because Becky is just one person.

RECOGNIZING PRONOUNS

A pronoun is used in place of a noun. It stands for the person, place, or thing the noun names.

Rules to Remember ✔

1. **Never use 's with possessive pronouns. They are already possessive.**

2. **Do not confuse reflexive and objective pronouns. Always use objective pronouns after prepositions and as receivers of verb action.**
   For example: The Mad Hatter gave the tea to Alice and me.
   Never: The Mad Hatter gave the tea to Alice and myself.

3. **Use reflexive pronouns to reflect only the person previously mentioned.**

Eight different kinds of pronouns are in the chart on the opposite page. Here you'll find examples of most of them.

The Secret Garden

She wished she could talk as he did. His speech was so quick and easy. It sounded as if he liked her and was not the least afraid she would not like him, though he was only a common moor boy, in patched clothes and with a funny face and a rough, rusty red head. As she came closer to him she noticed that there was a clean fresh scent of heather and grass and leaves about him, almost as if he were made of them. She liked it very much and when she looked into his funny face with the red cheeks and round blue eyes she forgot that she had felt shy.

PRONOUNS AND REFERENTS

When pronouns stand for something or someone we can refer back to, the thing the pronoun refers back to is called the referent.

Check out what can happen when the referent is unclear!

Rules to Remember

Pronouns used in sentences should be kept close to their referents. It should always be clear which person or thing the pronoun refers to.

Alice in Wonderland

". . . And even Stigand, the patriotic Archbishop of Canterbury, found it advisable—"

"Found what?" said the Duck.

"Found it," the Mouse replied rather crossly. "Of course, you know what 'it' means."

"I know what 'it' means well enough, when I find a thing," said the Duck: "It's generally a frog or a worm. The question is, what did the Archbishop find?"

A HANDY PRONOUN CHART

1. **Subjective pronouns:** act as subjects of verbs or of sentences.
   I, you, she, he, it, we, they, who, that, these, those
   He said Mary could have a garden.

2. **Objective pronouns:** can receive the action of a verb and can be used following prepositions.
   me, you, her, him, it, us, them, whom
   Aunt Polly gave candy to *them*. The boys ate *it* quickly.

3. **Possessive pronouns:** show ownership or possession of something.
   my, mine, your, yours, her, hers, his, its, our, ours, their, theirs, whose
   This garden is *mine*.

4. **Plural pronouns:** refer to more than one person or thing.
   we, us, our, ours, you, your, yours, they, them, their, theirs
   The Queen of Hearts gave orders to *them*.

5. **Demonstrative pronouns:** point out specific things.
   this, that, these, those
   Those flowers are gorgeous.

6. **Relative pronouns:** relate or connect parts of sentences.
   that, what, which, who, whose, whoever, whom, whomever, whatever, whichever
   They told us the story *that* scared us to death.

7. **Reflexive pronouns:** refer back to the subject of the sentence.
   myself, yourself, himself, herself, itself, ourselves, yourselves, themselves
   They wanted to do it *themselves*.

8. **Indefinite pronouns:** are used when the specific person or thing they stand for is not known.
   someone, somebody, something, no one, nobody, nothing, any, anybody, anything, all, everyone, everybody, everything
   Someone took the candy, but *no one* said *anything*.

Practice Makes Perfect!

WORD FOR THE DAY

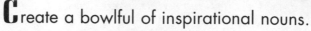

Create a bowlful of inspirational nouns.

WHAT YOU NEED: a sheet each of gold, white, black, and silver paper; scissors; paint markers; a decorative bowl or glass vase (big enough to get your hand in).

WHAT YOU DO: Make a list of inspirational nouns (nouns that give you an idea to think about). **Cut your colored paper** into strips big enough to fit a handwritten word. With your paint markers, **write one word** in neat cursive script or print per slip. **Mix the slips up** and put them in a bowl by the door. **Pull one out** as you leave each day and keep it with you to think about or share with a friend.

Some suggestions:

strength	happiness	peace	wisdom	memory
serenity	forgiveness	charm	beauty	wit
knowledge	discipline	compassion	discovery	luck
joy	wonder	dignity	magic	health

RECOGNIZING VERBS

Verbs tell what the subject does or is. Verbs are essential ingredients in sentences. Without them, it's like a cake made without flour—it doesn't hold together!

ACTION VERBS

A verb that describes something you can do is an action verb. Can you *sit, stand, sleep, talk, think, imagine, travel, drive, eat, write, play, throw, build, clean, climb, fold, drop, complain, scream, hop,* and *juggle*? These are all action verbs!

There can be doers of action and receivers of action. Just as in a football game, you can throw the ball or receive the ball. If the action happens to someone or something, it is the object of the action.

• •

Practice Makes Perfect!

PAPIER MÂCHÉ FRUIT AND FRUIT BOWL

Make a fabulous, decorative fruit bowl and all the fruit to go in it! Labeled with snappy action verbs related to preparing food, this will also dazzle with pictures of pies and other tempting fruit-filled treats.

WHAT YOU NEED: newspaper, magazines, wallpaper paste, vaseline or plastic wrap, scissors, four to six balloons of different sizes, decoupage glue, silver or gold paint marker, bowl.

WHAT YOU DO: Blow up the balloons to form the shapes of the fruits. (Use a long, thin balloon for a banana, an oval one for a pear, and round ones for apples and oranges.) **Cut or tear the newspaper** into 1½-inch-wide strips. **Mix the wallpaper paste** in a bowl. **Dip the paper strips** completely into the paste. **Cover each balloon** with at least two layers of newspaper strips, and smooth out any wrinkles. **Set the balloons aside** to dry overnight. To make your fruit bowl, **place a bowl upside down** on a firm surface. **Coat the bowl** with vaseline or plastic wrap to make it easier to separate later. **Dip more strips** into the wallpaper paste. To form a papier mâché bowl, **place at least two layers** of the coated newspaper strips over the bowl. **Smooth each layer. Set the bowl aside** to dry overnight. When dry, carefully

separate the papier mâché bowl from the bowl underneath. If necessary, **trim the edges** of your new bowl. Now you're ready to give your fruit and bowl action! **Decorate the dry fruit shapes and bowl** with colorful magazine pictures that show a treat made with each fruit, such as a banana

split, peach pie, apple cobbler, or grape jam. **Then add action verbs** related to preparing foods. **Cut these out of magazines** or write them on pieces of paper; then **attach them with glue.** Think of words that relate to each fruit. Here are some ideas:

> Banana—peel, bake, freeze, slice, mash.
>
> Apple—core, chop, dice.
>
> Orange—juice, peel, grate, drink.
>
> Pear—slice, puree, poach.
>
> Bowl—remove, dust, fill, cook, pour, press, bake, roll, sprinkle, coat, cool, mix, stir, spread, serve.

Paint on a thin coat of decoupage glue to cover.

• •

LINKING VERBS

A verb that tells what the subject is, is like, or seems to be is a linking verb. One of the most common linking verbs is *to be*. Its tenses are *am, is, are, was, were,* and *been*. Other linking verbs include *seem, appear,* and *feel*.

HINT ON FINDING LINKING VERBS or ACTION VERBS: If the verb answers what the subject *does,* it's an action verb. If the verb answers what the subject *is* or how it *seems,* it's a linking verb.

Linking verbs do not have receivers of their actions. They have complements instead. A complement is the word used after a linking verb to tell what the subject is or is like: Alice is a girl. Alice is curious.

In this excerpt below, Tom Sawyer must paint a fence before he is free to play. His life at the moment is not a happy one.

The Adventures of Tom Sawyer

Life to him seemed hollow, and existence [seemed] but a burden.

Life and *hollow* mean the same thing to Tom. They are linked by the linking verb *seemed*. *Existence* and *burden* also mean the same thing to Tom. *Hollow* is the complement of *life*. *Burden* is the complement of *existence*.

HELPING VERBS

Helping verbs "help" other verbs express the time of their action. Helping verbs join other verbs to tell what is happening, did happen, will happen, or might happen. They include *is, be, am, are, was, were, been, has, have, had, do, does, did, can, could, shall, should, will, would, may, might, must,* and *being.*

Rules to Remember ✔

Verbs agree in number with the subject, being singular or plural depending on the number of people or things in the subject. They do not agree with their objects or complements.

Even Twain Breaks the Rules

Aunt Polly, musing to herself because Tom has outwitted her once again: *"Ain't he played me tricks enough like that for me to be looking out for him by this time? But old fools is the biggest fools there is."*

What's wrong with the second sentence? It should say, "But old fools *are* the biggest fools there *are.*" Mark Twain knew this, but he wanted his characters to express themselves in the way they would in real life. So, he had Aunt Polly speak incorrect grammar!

VERB PARTS

INFINITIVES

Infinitives are the basic form of verbs preceded by *to*. Every verb has one of these infinitives—no matter what verb you think of—for example, *to play, to work, to sit, to plan, to eat*.

The verbs *am, is, are, was, were,* and *been* all come from the infinitive *to be. Do, does, did,* and *done* come from the infinitive *to do*.

VERB TENSE

Verb tense tells when the being or action occurred. If it already happened, the past verb tense is used. If it is happening now or is ongoing, the present tense is used. The future tense is used for things that will happen sometime in the future.

PARTICIPLES

Participles are used with helping verbs to form verb tenses. The *present participle* ends in *ing* and marks the action as immediate, or happening now. The *past participle*, ending in *ed* or *en*, shows that an action has been completed or will be completed. The simple past tense also ends in *ed*. The past tense of *start* is *started*. So is the past participle, but with *has, have,* or *had* before the verb.

On pages 23 through 25 you'll find a chart showing how present and past participles are used with helping verbs to tell the time of an action.

Jack London uses the helping verbs *was* and *were* with the present participle form of action verbs to describe the coming of spring in the Yukon at the time of the gold rush.

The Call of the Wild

*The sap was **rising** in the pines. The willows and aspens were **bursting** out in young buds. Shrubs and vines were **putting** on fresh garbs of green . . . Partridges and woodpeckers were **booming** and **knocking** in the forests. Squirrels were **chattering**, birds **singing**, and overhead honked the wild fowl **driving** up from the south in cunning wedges that split the air.*

The present participles are the bolded verbs that end in *ing*. Watch out! *Cunning* is not a verb. (It is an adjective used to describe *wedges*.)

Regular Past Tense

The regular past tense of verbs is created by adding *ed* to the present tense. It shows that the action already took place.

The Adventures of Tom Sawyer

His breath stopped and he listened. There was no sound— the stillness was perfect. His gratitude was measureless. Now he turned in his tracks . . . and then stepped quickly but cautiously along. When he emerged at the quarry he felt secure, and so he picked up his nimble feet and flew. Down, down he sped, till he reached the Welshman's. He banged at the door, and presently the heads of the old man and his two stalwart sons were thrust from the windows.

If it ends in *ed* and there is no helping verb in front of it, the verb is a regular past tense: *stopped, listened, turned, stepped, emerged, picked, reached,* and *banged* are the regular past tense verbs in the excerpt above.

Irregular Past Tense

Verbs whose past tenses are formed in ways other than by adding *ed* are called irregular. Examples are *fly/flew* and *drive/drove*.

This next excerpt includes the past tenses of these irregular verbs: *get, light, creep, stand, feel, begin, can, will, burst, find, come,* and *say.* Can you find each past tense?

The Adventures of Tom Sawyer

Tom got his lantern, lit it in the hogshead, wrapped it closely in the towel, and the two adventurers crept in the gloom toward the tavern. Huck stood sentry and Tom felt his way into the alley. Then there was a season of waiting anxiety that weighed upon Huck's spirit like a mountain. He began to wish he could see a flash from the lantern—it would frighten him, but it would at least tell him that Tom was alive yet. It seemed hours since Tom had disappeared. Surely he must have fainted; maybe he was dead; maybe his heart had burst under terror and excitement. In his uneasiness Huck found himself drawing closer and closer to the alley; fearing all sorts of dreadful things; and momentarily expecting some catastrophe to happen that would take away his breath. There was not much to take away, for he seemed only to inhale it by thimblefuls, and his heart would soon wear itself out, the way it was beating. Suddenly there was a flash of light and Tom came tearing by him: "Run!" said he; "run for your life!"

You are right if you picked *got, lit, crept, stood, felt, began, could, would, burst, found, came,* and *said.*

Here are some of the most used irregular verbs. This list will serve as a helpful reference for you.

IRREGULAR VERB CHART

Present Tense/ Present Participle	Past Tense	Past Participle (use with *has, have,* or *had*)
am, is, are/being	was, were	been
arise/arising	arose	arisen
bear/bearing	bore	born ["birth"]
		borne ["carried"]
beat/beating	beat	beaten
begin/beginning	began	begun
become/becoming	became	become
bid/bidding	bade	bidden
bite/biting	bit	bitten
blow/blowing	blew	blown
break/breaking	broke	broken
bring/bringing	brought	brought
burst/bursting	burst	burst
can [helping verb]	could	could (have)
catch/catching	caught	caught
choose/choosing	chose	chosen
come/coming	came	come
creep/creeping	crept	crept
deal/dealing	dealt	dealt
dig/digging	dug	dug
dive/diving	dove	dived
do/doing	did	done
draw/drawing	drew	drawn
drink/drinking	drank	drunk
drive/driving	drove	driven *(continued)*

Present Tense/ Present Participle	Past Tense	Past Participle (use with *has, have,* or *had*)
eat/eating	ate	eaten
fall/falling	fell	fallen
feed/feeding	fed	fed
feel/feeling	felt	felt
find/finding	found	found
fly/flying	flew	flown
forget/forgetting	forgot	forgotten
freeze/freezing	froze	frozen
get/getting	got	got, gotten
give/giving	gave	given
go/going	went	gone
grow/growing	grew	grown
hang/hanging	hung	hung
know/knowing	knew	known
lay/laying	laid	laid
lead/leading	led	led
leave/leaving	left	left
lend/lending	lent	lent
lie/lying	lay	lain
light/lighting	lit	lit
lose/losing	lost	lost
must [helping verb]	-----	must (have)
pay/paying	paid	paid
ride/riding	rode	ridden
ring/ringing	rang	rung
run/running	ran	run
say/saying	said	said

Present Tense/ Present Participle	Past Tense	Past Participle (use with *has, have,* or *had*)
see/seeing	saw	seen
send/sending	sent	sent
set/setting	set	set
shake/shaking	shook	shaken
shrink/shrinking	shrank	shrunk
sing/singing	sang	sung
sink/sinking	sank	sunk
sit/sitting	sat	sat
speak/speaking	spoke	spoken
spin/spinning	spun	spun
spring/springing	sprang	sprung
stand/standing	stood	stood
steal/stealing	stole	stolen
stick/sticking	stuck	stuck
strike/striking	struck	struck, (was) stricken
swear/swearing	swore	sworn
swim/swimming	swam	swum
take/taking	took	taken
tear/tearing	tore	torn
tell/telling	told	told
throw/throwing	threw	thrown
wake/waking	woke, waked	woken, waked
wear/wearing	wore	worn
will [helping verb]	would	would (have)
wind/winding	wound	wound
wring/wringing	wrung	wrung
write/writing	wrote	written

Verbals

Verbals are infinitives and participles, formed from verbs, that are used as other parts of speech.

For example, in these sentences, both the present participle and the infinitive act as nouns:

Fishing is a great pastime for kids. Tom loves to fish.

Here, *fishing* is the subject of the first sentence, and *to fish* is the object of the second sentence.

Present Participles and Gerunds

When a present participle is used as a noun, it is called a gerund.

This quotation contains several gerunds, as well as present participles that show the time of action. See if you can tell which is which.

Alice in Wonderland

Alice went timidly up to the door, and knocked.
"There's no sort of use in knocking," said the Footman, "and that for two reasons. First, because I'm on the same side of the door as you are: secondly, because they're making such a noise inside, no one could possibly hear you." And certainly there was a most extraordinary noise going on within—a constant howling and sneezing, and every now and then a great crash, as if a dish or kettle had been broken to pieces.

There are four present participles in this quote: *knocking, making, howling,* and *sneezing.* The present participle verb is *making.* The others are gerunds because they are naming things, which means they are used as nouns.

CONTRACTIONS

A contraction is a word made from two words, one of which has been shortened by leaving out some letters and putting in an apostrophe to take their place.

Alice in Wonderland

"Look out now, Five! Don't go splashing paint over me like that!"

"I couldn't help it," said Five, in a sulky tone. "Seven jogged my elbow." On which Seven looked up and said, "That's right, Five. Always lay the blame on others!" "You'd better not talk!" said Five. "I heard the Queen say only yesterday you deserved to be beheaded."

"What for?" said the one who had spoken first.

"That's none of your business, Two!" said Seven.

"Yes, it is his business!" said Five. "And I'll tell him—it was for bringing the cook tulip-roots instead of onions."

Many contractions were used in this passage. Do you know how they're made?

○ *don't* comes from *do not*.
○ *couldn't* comes from *could not*.
○ *that's* comes from *that is*.
○ *you'd* comes from *you had*.
○ *I'll* comes from *I will*.

Rules to Remember

Do not confuse these pronoun contractions with possessive pronouns:

contractions	possessive pronouns
it is = it's	its (belonging to it)
they are = they're	their (belonging to them)
you are = you're	your (belonging to you)
who is = who's	whose (asks or tells to whom something belongs)

Hint: **Contractions have apostrophes in place of missing letters; possessive pronouns do not.**

RECOGNIZING ADJECTIVES

Adjectives add detail to nouns or pronouns so that it is possible to know which person or thing is being talked about. Adjectives often tell which one, what kind, or how many. They point out such things as size, color, shape, ownership, and position.

Sometimes adjectives describe nouns to create a picture of them in your mind.

A butterfly can be described simply as "a bug," but it's described much more clearly by telling what it looks like. For example:

The beautiful blue and purple striped butterfly is on the yellow flower.

Now you try it.

Put five boxes on a table and ask for one. When someone gives you one, say, "No, not that one." The person gives you another one, and again it is the wrong one. Keep doing this until the other person gets frustrated and yells, "Tell me which one you mean!" How would you tell your frustrated friend which one?

Each box would need to be different so you could ask for it using a certain description. For example, you could have a flat box, a pink box, a round box, a wooden box, and an open box. *Flat, pink, round, wooden,* and *open* all tell what kind of boxes you have. These adjectives tell the boxes apart.

In the following two excerpts, you will see how adjectives are used to describe two people by their very different characteristics. First a description of Mary, as she was at the beginning of the book:

The Secret Garden

Everybody said she was the most disagreeable-looking child ever seen. It was true, too. She had a little thin face and a little thin body, thin light hair and a sour expression.

Next, a description of Mary's mother:

[She] was such a tall, slim, pretty person and wore such lovely clothes. Her hair was like curly silk and she had a delicate little nose which seemed to be disdaining things, and she had large, laughing eyes.

Did Mary look like her mother? Which words helped make a picture in your mind of Mary and her mother? These are adjectives.

You are right if you picked the following descriptive words about Mary: *most disagreeable-looking* (child); *little thin* (face); *little thin* (body); *thin light* (hair); *sour* (expression). These are the descriptive words used for her mother: *tall, slim, pretty* (person); *lovely* (clothes); *her* (hair); *curly* (silk); *delicate little* (nose); *large, laughing* (eyes).

• •

Practice Makes Perfect!

ADD UP THE SALES

Create an advertisement to "sell" your product, using the most descriptive adjectives you can find.

WHAT YOU NEED: magazine pictures and words, scissors, glue stick, 11-by-14-inch blank poster board.

WHAT YOU DO: Pick an object to describe in your ad. The more unusual the object is, the harder it will be to find just the right words to describe it. Then **select descriptive adjectives** from magazines that will help you "sell" your product. Be creative! **Draw or paste a picture**

BUY YOUR OWN SCARECROW!

of the object on the poster board. This is the beginning of your ad. **Arrange the descriptive** adjectives around it so that it looks like an ad from a magazine. You can also **write your own words** on slips of paper. Do the words you have chosen sell your product? (If you are coming up with your own words, a thesaurus is a great reference tool to use!)

• •

POSSESSIVES USED AS ADJECTIVES

Possessive nouns and pronouns are used as adjectives when they describe an object by indicating ownership. Here are examples:

The Adventures of Tom Sawyer

During three days Tom was deeply concerned about the judge's condition and hungry for news of it.
　　There were some boys-and-girls' parties, but they were so few and so delightful that they only made the aching voids between ache the harder.

In these sentences, the possessive *judge's* describes the noun *condition*, letting the reader know whose condition. The reader also knows what kind of parties there were because *boys-and-girls'* describes the parties.

PRESENT AND PAST PARTICIPLES USED AS ADJECTIVES

Present and past participles can be adjectives when they are used to describe.

The Adventures of Tom Sawyer

And that night there came a terrific storm, with driving rain, awful claps of thunder, and blinding sheets of lightning.

Notice how the rain and sheets of lightning are described. There are three words that end in *ing* in the sentence above. One is a noun. The other two are adjectives. Can you tell which ones? Ask: What kind of rain? What kind of sheets? The present participles *driving* and *blinding* give the answers. *Lightning* is the noun.

The Call of the Wild

Spitz struggled madly to keep up. He saw the silent circle, with gleaming eyes, lolling tongues, and silvery breaths drifting upward, closing in upon him as he had seen similar circles close in upon beaten antagonists in the past.

Jack London used the following adjectives: *silent, gleaming, lolling, silvery, similar, beaten.* Can you identify the two present participles used as adjectives? (Hint: They end in *ing*.) The past participle *beaten* is used as an adjective to describe *antagonists*.

RECOGNIZING ADVERBS

An adverb describes a verb, another adverb, or an adjective by telling where, when, or how, and to what extent.

Adverbs often end in *ly*. For example: *softly, quietly, loudly, quickly, awkwardly,* and *usually.* Without the *ly* each of these words is an adjective.

Let's say you were invited to a magic show. It was so amazing that you couldn't wait to get home and tell everyone about it. But let's also say that you couldn't use any adverbs. Do you see how it might become very difficult to describe your exciting adventure without using any words that tell how, when, or where the magician performed?

NEGATIVE ADVERBS

These are considered negative adverbs: *barely, scarcely, rarely,* and *never.* It is important to remember that they are negative, so you should not use them with a negative verb.

Notice the adverbs in the example below. Then take a look at the chart showing how they function in each sentence.

The Secret Garden

One knows it sometimes when one gets up at the tender solemn dawn-time and goes out and stands alone and throws one's head far back and looks up and up and watches the pale sky slowly changing and flushing and marvelous unknown things happening until the East almost makes one cry out and one's heart stands still at the strange unchanging majesty of the rising sun—which has been happening every morning for thousands and thousands and thousands of years.

Rules to Remember ✔

Do not use a negative adverb (*never*) with a negative verb (*didn't*). Two negatives cancel each other out and change the meaning from negative to positive! Don't say, "He didn't never give me a chance" unless you mean "He did give me a chance." (And if that is what you mean, say it the way that is more clear!)

ADVERBS AND WHAT THEY MODIFY

Adverb	Word Modified	How the Adverb Modifies It
sometimes	knows	tells *when*
out	goes	tells *where*
alone	stands	tells *how*
back	throws	tells *where*
far	back	tells *to what extent*
up and up	looks	tells *where*
slowly	changing and flushing	tells *how*
almost	makes	tells *to what degree*, or *how much*
still	stands	tells *how*

Practice Makes Perfect!

THE GREAT GRAMMAR GARDEN

Do you have a green thumb? Even if you don't, you can make this beautiful indoor/outdoor garden labeled with nouns and adjectives on garden markers.

WHAT YOU NEED: potting soil; plants or seeds; Popsicle® sticks; clay you can bake in an oven; paints or paint markers; pot, glass bowl, or aquarium (optional).

WHAT YOU DO: The garden you make can be a garden plot in the ground, in a pot or terrarium in the house, or even in a bag of potting soil on a patio. **Decide on a theme** for your garden. Possibilities include: a flower garden, an edible garden, a container garden, a garden of desert plants, and a garden of oddities (plants that move when touched, plants that eat insects, etc.). **Make a list** of nouns and adjectives to describe the plants in your garden. You can use the plants' known names (Coreopsis Giganticus, Ice Rose) or make up your own names for them (Jeff's Giant Pandas). **Add descriptive adjectives** for each plant, based on what they do or how they look. Now you're ready to make your garden markers. **Form the clay** around Popsicle® sticks. **Flatten the sides and bake** according to the directions on the package. You can **use waterproof paints or markers** to decorate the clay once it cools. Or, before you bake the clay, **scratch the names and designs** into the garden markers.

COMPARATIVES AND SUPERLATIVES

You may not realize it, but you probably use comparatives and superlatives every day, maybe in every conversation! Every time you talk about who is taller than so-and-so, who can run fastest or yell the loudest, or who the best football player is, you use a comparative or superlative. So what are they?

When two things are compared, the comparative form of an adjective or adverb is used to show that one thing has more of the quality than the other does. When more than two things are compared, the superlative form is used to tell which has the most of the quality the adjective or adverb describes.

Alice in Wonderland

"Curiouser and curiouser!" cried Alice (she was so much surprised, that for the moment she quite forgot how to speak good English).

Don't be like Alice. Learn to make comparatives and superlatives.

Here are four ways to make comparative and superlative adjectives and adverbs:

1. Comparatives are made by adding *er* to the basic adjective or adverb, and superlatives are made by adding *est* to the basic word. This is the rule when the adjectives or adverbs are regular in form and not more than two syllables in length. For example: *tall/taller/tallest; easy/easier/easiest; big/bigger/biggest; smart/smarter/smartest.*

2. When adjectives and adverbs are more than two syllables in length, use *more* in front of the basic word to make the comparative and *most* to make the superlative. Alice should have said, "More and more curious!" The comparative form of *curious* is *more curious*; the superlative form is *most curious.* Other examples are: *inquisitive/more inquisitive/most inquisitive; awkwardly/more awkwardly/most awkwardly.*

Rules to Remember ✔

Never use both methods of making comparatives or superlatives. For example, do not say, "He had the most ugliest temper you could ever imagine." ***Ugliest* is the correct superlative form to use.**

3. Adjectives and adverbs may be compared by being less, rather than more, of their quality. In such a case, the comparison would be, for example: *less awkwardly/least awkwardly.*

4. Comparatives and superlatives also have irregular forms, which should be memorized. They are: *good/better/best; bad/worse/worst; less/lesser/least; some/more/most.*

• •

Practice Makes Perfect!

THE BEST MOBILE EVER

You can have fun creating an awesome moving display that shows basic adjectives with their comparatives and superlatives.

WHAT YOU NEED: magazines, markers, glue stick, scissors, fishing line, screw-in ceiling hooks, light cardboard, hole puncher, colored paper, fabric scraps, glitter (optional).

WHAT YOU DO: To begin building your mobile, **find three pictures:** a basic adjective (*big*), a comparative (*bigger*), and a superlative (*biggest*). Flip through magazines, take photographs, create your own drawings, or mix and match—it's your choice! You'll want to find at least four sets of adjectives, twelve pictures in all. **Paste each picture** on a piece of 2-by-2-inch light cardboard. **Decorate with fabric scraps,** or glitter if you wish. **Label the pictures** with the basic, comparative, and superlative word forms. Then **assemble**. Each fishing line will contain three cards—an adjective in its three forms. **Lay the first three squares** vertically facedown on a table. **Take three more squares** and glue them faceup on top of the first three. **Punch holes** in the top and bottom of the top two squares and a hole in the top only of the bottom square. With fishing line, **tie them together** with about an inch of space between each. **Repeat** with the rest of your squares. Finally, **attach the fishing lines** to a hanger or a stick, and hang the mobile from your ceiling!

• •

RECOGNIZING PREPOSITIONS

Prepositions connect nouns or pronouns with other words in a sentence. Prepositions are "going places" words. They help the nouns or pronouns that follow them, telling where something has taken place or when, where, or why things have been done.

They played the game <u>at recess</u>. They rested <u>after lunch</u>. She baked the cake <u>for me</u>.

Many prepositions establish what is called spatial relationships—they help make clear where events happen in and through space.

The Call of the Wild

It was a hard day's run, up the Canyon, through Sheep Camp, past the Scales and the timber line, across glaciers and snowdrifts hundreds of feet deep, and over the great Chilkoot Divide, which stands between the salt water and the fresh and guards forbiddingly the sad and lonely North. They made good time down the chain of lakes which fills the crater of extinct volcanoes, and late that night pulled into the huge camp at the head of Lake Bennett, where thousands of gold seekers were building boats against the break-up of the ice in the spring. Buck made his hole in the snow and slept the sleep of the exhausted just, but all too early was routed out in the cold darkness and harnessed with his mates to the sled.

The prepositions that help explain where events happened are: *up, through, past, across, over, between, down, into, at, out, in,* and *to.* Can you visualize the dogs pulling the sled and moving through the icy, cold space described in the story?

Practice Makes Perfect!

PREPOSITION TREASURE HUNT

You can play this fun treasure hunt game with one friend or a whole group.

WHAT YOU NEED: paper, scissors, pen, small objects to match word list.

WHAT YOU DO: Make a list of spatial relationships (where things are located in relationship to one another). These of course include prepositions. Examples are "in the room," "next to the box," "under the paper," and "in front of the fence." **Write these** on slips of paper. Then **make a list of objects** you have on hand, such as a spoon, ticket, pencil, and crayon. **Hide the objects,** using your list of spatial relationships as your guide. (Hide the spoon "next to the box," and put the ticket "under the paper.") **Write their location** next to the list of objects

and tack this list up where it can be seen by all players. Have the players run out, find an object, and return to see what's next on the list. The first one to find the most is the winner.

• •

RECOGNIZING CONJUNCTIONS

Conjunctions join sentences or parts of sentences. Sometimes people or things have to be together to accomplish their mission, like a team of astronauts blasting off to Mars. Sometimes parts of sentences have to be partnered, or joined together, too. Either they join together to do the same thing in the sentence, or they add something that is needed to make the sentence's message more clear.

These conjunctions are joining words: *and, but, or, for, yet, so,* and *nor.* They are called coordinating conjunctions because they coordinate, or combine, parts of sentences so they can do their work together. Here's how.

If more than one person, place, or thing is the topic of the sentence, these two (or more) subjects can be joined by a conjunction to become a compound subject. If the subject does more than one action, the verbs can be joined to become a compound verb. Other parts of speech can be joined to become compounds.

The Call of the Wild

That winter, at Dawson, Buck performed another exploit, not so heroic, perhaps, **but** *one that put his name many notches higher on the totem pole of Alaskan fame. This exploit was particularly gratifying to the three men;* **for** *they stood in need of the outfit which it furnished,* **and** *were enabled to make a long-desired trip to the virgin East, where miners had not yet appeared.*

You can see how Jack London used conjunctions to put ideas and parts of sentences together in the excerpt above.

Only the bolded words are conjunctions. Other words you might see on a list of conjunctions are not used as such here. The *so* in the first sentence is an adjective that tells how heroic. The *yet* in the last sentence is an adverb that tells when the miners had not appeared.

HINT ON HUNTING CONJUNCTIONS: It is not a conjunction unless it joins parts of speech or sections of a sentence.

As Jack London describes the dog Buck in the following excerpt, *yet* is used as a conjunction because it joins two parts of the sentence, showing us that the dog has two different kinds of characteristics.

The Call of the Wild

Faithfulness and devotion; things born of fire and roof, were his; **yet** *he retained his wildness and wiliness.*

The conjunction *and* is used three times in the sentence to join things that equal each other: *faithfulness and devotion, fire and roof,* and *wildness and wiliness.*

For appears twice in this selection from Lewis Carroll. One is a conjunction, and one is a preposition. See if you can tell which is which.

Alice in Wonderland

"Please would you tell me," said Alice, a little timidly, **for** she was not quite sure whether it was good manners **for** her to speak first, *"why your cat grins like that?"*

HINT ON HUNTING CONJUNCTIONS AND PREPOSITIONS: To choose the conjunction, think of *for* as meaning "because." Remember, a conjunction **joins** and a preposition **introduces** a noun or pronoun.

• •

Practice Makes Perfect!

THE SINGSONG SHOWDOWN

Got a frog in your throat? Let him out by playing Singsong Showdown, using adjectives, verbs, adverbs, nouns, and comparatives and superlatives! This game for two or more will challenge your creativity as you take turns making up a poem, song, or rhyme.

WHAT YOU NEED: paper, pencil.

WHAT YOU DO: Each team will **make a list** of ten words in each of the following categories: comparatives and superlatives, nouns (don't forget to throw in some proper nouns, the sillier the better!), adjectives, verbs, and adverbs. **Exchange your 50-word list** with the other team. Each team then **makes up a poem,** rhyme, or song using as many of

the words on the list as possible. **Set a time limit** and let the creative juices loose! Whoever uses the most words properly wins.

• •

RECOGNIZING INTERJECTIONS

Interjections add strong feeling or emotion to what is being said, yet they are not necessary parts of a sentence.

HINT ON HUNTING INTERJECTIONS: You can see how interjections work by taking them out of a sentence. Notice how, when they are gone, the meaning of the sentence does not change. What does change? Emotion is lost. Interjections express feelings such as surprise, anger, sorrow, or happiness.

The Adventures of Tom Sawyer

Hang the boy, *can't I never learn anything? . . . But* **my goodness,** *he never plays them alike, two days, and how is a body to know what's coming? . . . I ain't doing my duty by that boy, and that's the Lord's truth,* **goodness knows.** *. . . He's full of the Old Scratch, but* **laws-a-me!** *he's my own dead sister's boy,* **poor thing,** *and I ain't got the heart to lash him, somehow. . . .* **Well-a-well** *. . .*

Aunt Polly has been calling for Tom with no answer. Tom is hiding in the closet, eating the jam Aunt Polly was preserving for the winter. When Aunt Polly discovers him, she scolds him and tells him to hand her a switch, a small flexible branch, so that she can smack him. But Tom tricks Aunt Polly and escapes. As Aunt Polly begins musing, we notice the interjections throughout her thoughts.

Other interjections commonly used are *aw, wow, yippee,* and *boo.*

Just as carpenters have their hammers and artists their paints, you now have all the parts of speech tools you need to build sentences. Let's go ahead and have some fun with them!

Practice Makes Perfect!

THE MOST AND LEAST GAME

This fun game will give you practice identifying the parts of speech. You can play alone or with your whole class!

WHAT YOU NEED: lively, colorful magazine or newspaper ads (one per player), pen or colored pencil (one per player).

WHAT YOU DO: Each player gets one ad. Players get up to five minutes to **read through the ad** and **label the parts of speech** according to the point code below. (Player with the most points wins.)

nouns – 1 point   adjectives – 3 points   prepositions – 5 points

verbs – 2 points   adverbs – 4 points   pronouns – 6 points

conjunctions – 2 points   interjections – 10 points

Building a sentence is like building a hamburger. A hamburger can be okay with just two parts: a plain bun and meat patty. But add ketchup, mayonnaise, mustard, pickles, relish, lettuce, tomatoes, cheese on the patty, and sesame seeds on the bun—now, THAT'S a hamburger!

A sentence must have two parts: a subject and a predicate. The subject is the person or thing the sentence *is about,* and the predicate tells what the subject *does* or *is.*

A sentence can be as simple as its basic two parts—a subject and a verb—or it can be "superdeluxe," like that hamburger with all the trimmings. Want to build a superdeluxe sentence? Take your basic subject (topic) and predicate (what happens), and add adjectives, adverbs, and other parts of speech to tell more about the subject and predicate and turn the sentence into something that really has zing.

SENTENCE TYPES

1. A declarative sentence makes a statement, telling facts or information.
2. An interrogative sentence asks a question, requesting information or answers.
3. An exclamatory sentence exclaims, expressing emphasis or surprise about something.
4. An imperative sentence gives an order or makes a request. If the sentence is a command to do something and be quick about it, an exclamation point will probably appear at the end. If the sentence is a polite request, it will end with a period.
5. A negative sentence tells or asks what did *not* happen, emphasizing the *not*.

Through the Looking Glass

"I see nobody on the road," said Alice.

"I only wish I had such eyes," the King remarked in a fretful tone. "To be able to see Nobody! And at that distance too! Why, it's as much as I can do to see real people, by this light!"

Lewis Carroll created humor from the King's confusion over Alice's use of a positive verb and negative pronoun. Although Alice was speaking correctly, the confusion could have been avoided if she had said, "I don't see anybody." But then there would have been no joke!

Did you notice the exclamatory sentences the King used? He was exclaiming to emphasize his amazement.

Following is a conversation between Alice and the Red Queen. See if you can read it with the expression in your voice that goes with each sentence type.

Through the Looking Glass

"Where do you come from?" . . . *"And where are you going?"* (interrogative)

"Look up, speak nicely, and don't twiddle your fingers all the time." (imperative)

Alice attended to all these directions and explained, as well as she could, that she had lost her way. (declarative)

"I don't know what you mean by your *way."* (negative) *"All the ways about here belong to* me—*but why did you come out here at all?" she added in a kinder tone. "Curtsy while you're thinking what to say."* (imperative)

SENTENCE MOODS

There is one more thing that affects sentences and the expression in the voice when speaking them, and that is mood, or form of expression.

The indicative mood indicates how things actually are. It is the mood that verbs usually express. Declarative sentences stating facts are in the indicative mood.

The imperative mood is used with imperative sentences.

The subjunctive mood is used with sentences that wish things were different or describe things as they really aren't. The use of the subjunctive mood to express conditions contrary to fact requires a different form of the verb *to be* than the use of the indicative does. For example, do not say: "If I *was* you, I would go." Say: "If I *were* you, I would go." Do not say: " I wish I *was* home right now." Say: "I wish I *were* home right now."

● ●

Practice Makes Perfect!

TREAT YOURSELF TO A SENTENCE TYPE!

Enjoy a treat and at the same time learn how to write up your favorite snack recipe, using the different sentence types. You can either make up a recipe or use one of your old favorites to inspire you.

WHAT YOU NEED: a pencil or pen, paper or 5-by-7-inch index card. (If you want to whip up—and eat—the snack, you'll need the ingredients for that, too!)

WHAT YOU DO: Find a recipe you enjoy or come up with an

original one. Then, using the five sentence types on page 44, **write out the steps of the recipe** one by one on a 5-by-7-inch index card or sheet of paper trimmed to a 5-by-7-inch size. Once you've finished, at the top of the card or paper, write your own name for the recipe—one that reminds you of the dish! See the sample below.

Crazy, Cheesy Cinnamon Apple Pie Rounds

Preheat the oven to 350 degrees. Place six rounds of biscuit dough on a pan. Sprinkle rounds with ½ teaspoon cinnamon. Dip cut-up apple slices in water mixed with 1 teaspoon lemon juice. Place the slices on top of the biscuit rounds. Spoon apple pie filling on top of each round. Do you like nutmeg? If you do, sprinkle with ¼ teaspoon nutmeg. Place a piece of sharp cheddar cheese on top of each. (Low-fat cheddar cheese can be substituted.) Slide the pan into the oven and bake for ten minutes or until the biscuit dough is cooked thoroughly and the cheese is melted and toasty. Yum! Carefully remove the pan from the oven and allow to cool. Don't burn yourself!

SENTENCE STRUCTURE

Sentences can be put together in layers, the way that cakes are. They may be simple one-layer sentences, like a sheet cake. They may be compound, like a two-layer birthday cake, or complex, like a fancy, many-layered wedding cake.

Parts of sentences called clauses define the structure of sentences as simple, compound, or complex.

A clause is a group of words containing a subject and a predicate, which tells what the subject does or is. Clauses may be independent or dependent.

INDEPENDENT CLAUSE

When a clause can stand alone to express a complete thought, it is called an independent clause. In the following selection, Tom is showing his treasures in an effort to make a trade:

The Adventures of Tom Sawyer

Tom exhibited. They were satisfactory, and the property changed hands.

This selection contains three independent clauses. Each has a subject (in bold) and a predicate (underlined), and each expresses a complete idea: 1. **Tom** exhibited. 2. **They** were satisfactory. 3. **The property** changed hands.

DEPENDENT CLAUSE

A dependent clause is a group of words, including at least a subject and a predicate, that acts as the subject, object, or modifier of the rest of the sentence. It must have the rest of the sentence to complete a thought.

Dependent clauses sometimes introduce an idea, and then leave the reader or listener waiting to hear the rest of the sentence, as in this excerpt:

The Adventures of Tom Sawyer

When they came to recite their lessons, not one of them knew his verses perfectly, but had to be prompted all along.

The dependent clause is *When they came to recite their lessons.* It is a clause because it is a group of related words containing a subject (*they*) and a predicate (*came to recite their lessons*). It is dependent because it doesn't complete the idea of the sentence. Such a clause is called a sentence fragment. It starts out to tell you something but doesn't finish.

Practice Makes Perfect!

CARTOON CLIPS AND CAPERS

Want to have some fun with words? Get out your scissors, and snap open your newspaper to the comics section!

WHAT YOU NEED: scissors, glue stick, 3-by-5-inch note cards, newspaper comics (or comic books).

WHAT YOU DO: Write one of each of the five sentence types (see page 44) on the back of a blank note card. As you read the comics, look for speech balloons that feature each sentence type. **Clip the part of the cartoon** matching a sentence type, and **paste it on the front of that note card**. Now for the "funnies" stuff! **Rearrange your cards** so they're laid out in a line to make a new comic. Don't worry if you have snips from all sorts of different cartoons—the more the merrier!

SIMPLE SENTENCE

A simple sentence expresses a complete thought, using a single independent clause.

The Call of the Wild

"Gad, sir! Gad, sir!" sputtered the Skookum Bench king. "I'll give you a thousand for him, sir, a thousand, sir— twelve hundred, sir."

Thornton rose to his feet. His eyes were wet. The tears were streaming frankly down his cheeks. "Sir," he said to the Skookum Bench king, "no, sir."

In this scene, the Skookum Bench king wants to buy the dog, Buck, from Thornton, and Thornton says no. All the sentences in this excerpt are simple sentences, because they have one independent clause containing one subject noun or pronoun and one predicate verb. Each single clause expresses the whole idea of the sentence.

COMPOUND SENTENCE

A compound sentence is made up of two or more independent clauses joined by a conjunction. The clauses are equally important and could be separated into simple sentences. In this selection, Tom and Becky are looking for a spring with water they can drink:

The Adventures of Tom Sawyer

They found one presently, and Tom said it was time to rest again. Both were cruelly tired, yet Becky said she thought she could go on a little further.

The compound sentences in this excerpt could have been written as simple sentences:

They found one presently. Tom said it was time to rest again. Both were cruelly tired. Becky said she thought she could go on a little further.

Do the thoughts read better as two sentences or four?

● ●

Practice Makes Perfect!

SENTENCE ART-TEES

Want to dress up your wardrobe? Maybe make a statement? You'll end up with a fabulous T-shirt displaying your favorite quotes from the not-so-rich or famous.

WHAT YOU NEED: a T-shirt, newspaper or aluminum foil, fabric paint, paintbrush, fabric pens.

WHAT YOU DO: Choose a sentence, either complex or compound. It may be your own or one you have found that you think is funny or inspirational. For example: *If you can't say something nice, don't say anything at all.* If you quote directly from a book or movie, you should credit the author by adding his or her name below the sentence. To decorate your tee, **place it** flat on a surface and **slip some newspaper or foil inside** to keep paint from running through to the back. With paints or pens, **write the first clause** on the front of the shirt and the second on the back. Be sure to **allow your shirt to dry** before wearing it.

● ●

COMPLEX SENTENCE

A complex sentence contains at least one independent clause and one dependent clause. The dependent clause introduces the independent clause or adds to it to complete the thought of the sentence.

The Adventures of Tom Sawyer

When the ferryboat with her wild freight pushed into the stream, nobody cared sixpence for the wasted time but the captain of the craft.

Rules to Remember ✔

Always look for a subject and a predicate to identify a clause. It will be an independent clause if it expresses a complete thought. Dependent clauses, however, leave you needing more information. Sometimes a dependent clause shows up in the middle of an independent clause to provide information the reader needs right away.

The main clause of this sentence is *nobody cared sixpence for the wasted time but the captain of the craft.* The dependent clause is *when the ferryboat with her wild freight pushed into the stream.* The dependent clause introduces the main clause and tells the time of the action.

See if you can identify the independent and dependent clauses in the following sentence:

And now the tiresome chirping of a cricket, that no human ingenuity could locate, began.

The independent clause is: *and now the tiresome chirping of a cricket began.* The dependent clause is *that no human ingenuity could locate.* Here, the dependent clause divides the independent clause.

PUNCTUATION

Pretend you are a child actor who has just been chosen for the lead in a new sitcom. Once you stop screaming and jumping up and down for joy, you have to get down to business and read and memorize some scripts.

You begin to read, and as you do, you keep seeing a little symbol that shows when the audience will be told to laugh. But what shows *you* how to say your lines? Punctuation, specific marks in written communication used to signal the reader, shows you how to slow down, pause, raise your voice, drop your voice, or add pizzazz—emphasis and excitement!

Punctuation marks include capital letter, period, question mark, exclamation point, comma, semicolon, colon, ellipsis points, apostrophe, quotation marks, and parentheses.

CAPITAL LETTER

A capital letter signals importance. It is the leader of a sentence. When should you use a capital letter?

1. Use a capital to signal the beginning of a sentence. Look at this sentence:

   gardens need water, sunlight, and love to grow.

   You can't tell that the sentence has begun!
   Use the capital letter to begin:

   Gardens need water, sunlight, and love to grow.

2. Use a capital to signal a proper noun. Proper nouns name particular people, places, languages, books, movies, and so on.

   Jack London wrote The Call of the Wild, which takes place in Alaska.

3. The pronoun *I* should always be capitalized.

PERIOD

A period at the end of a sentence signals that it is finished. Periods are also used with abbreviations to signal that a word has been shortened.

Names of states and titles are often abbreviated: Mo. (Missouri), Mr. (Mister), Rev. (Reverend), Capt. (Captain). Also: St. (Street), Ave. (Avenue), and so on.

Months are often abbreviated: Jan., Feb., Mar., Apr., Aug., Sept., Oct., Nov., Dec.

Don't forget the abbreviations for the days of the week: Sun., Mon., Tues., Wed., Thu., Fri., Sat.

QUESTION MARK

A question mark signals that information is being requested, rather than being stated.

The Secret Garden

"How old are you?" he asked.
"I am ten," answered Mary, forgetting herself for the moment, "and so are you."
"How do you know that?" he demanded in a surprised voice.
"Because when you were born the garden door was locked and the key was buried. And it has been locked for ten years."

Mary and Colin are just getting to know each other in this conversation. Notice the question marks that end the two sentences asking for information.

EXCLAMATION POINT

An exclamation point is used at the end of a sentence to signal surprise or emphasis.

The Secret Garden

". . . I'm well! I'm well! I feel—I feel as if I want to shout out something—something thankful, joyful!"

Exclamation points are also often used after interjections: Dear me! Oh, my! My goodness! Great! Gee whiz!

COMMA

A comma signals a pause within a sentence. Commas group words that belong together and separate them from the rest of the sentence. Use commas when the reader might have difficulty telling what the meaning is without them. But do not confuse the meaning by putting in more commas than are needed. When should you use a comma?

1. Use a comma after introductory words, phrases, or clauses.

2. Use a comma when several items are listed in a series.

3. Use a comma when two independent clauses are joined by coordinating conjunctions, such as *but, and, or,* or *for.*

4. Use a comma when inserting words such as *unfortunately, however, nevertheless, inasmuch as, namely, for example, that is,* and *especially* in a sentence and interrupting its thought. Commas are also needed when inserting descriptive phrases between a subject and its predicate.

   In this excerpt, Tom is having difficulty getting up his courage to testify in court about a murder:

The Adventures of Tom Sawyer

The audience listened breathless, but the words refused to come. After a few moments, however, the boy got a

little of his strength back, and managed to put enough of it into his voice to make part of the house hear: "In the graveyard!"

Can you see how commas and the use of *however* help the author express the change in Tom?

The master, throned on high in his great splint-bottom armchair, was dozing, lulled by the drowsy hum of study.

Notice how the schoolmaster is pictured more clearly by the addition of descriptive phrases, which are set off by commas.

5. Use commas within dates (January 14, 1987), addresses (196 Maple Street, Madison, Wisconsin), and numbers over one thousand (1,346).

Because it is easy to overuse commas, it is as important to know when not to use commas as it is to know when to use them. When not to use a comma:

1. Do not use commas when the thought is intended to be completed without any interruption.

2. Do not use a comma between a verb and its object. For example: **Tom found a kite string in his pocket.** (If Tom found several items, however, separate the items by commas: **Tom found a kite string, some candles, and a piece of candy in his pocket.**)

3. Do not use commas when an independent clause (a complete thought) is followed by a dependent clause (an incomplete thought) that describes it.

Rules to Remember

Use commas in places where the reader might have difficulty telling what the meaning is without them. But do not confuse the meaning by putting in more commas than are needed.

The incomplete thought will usually tell when or why the clause expressing the complete thought happened, as in the following examples:

The Call of the Wild

Buck had been purposely placed between Dave and Sol-leks so that he might receive instruction.

No comma is used after Sol-leks because the dependent clause tells why Buck was placed between the other two dogs, and the thought should not be interrupted.

He learned to bite the ice out with his teeth when it collected between his toes . . .

No comma is used after *teeth* because the reader needs to know, without interruption, when in particular Buck bit the ice out with his teeth.

SEMICOLON

A semicolon signals a stronger pause than a comma. A semicolon separates items listed by groups, rather than singly. Items within the group are separated by commas, and then the groups themselves are separated by semicolons. Sometimes semicolons are used to connect related thoughts instead of using the conjunctions *for, so, and, but, or,* or *nor.*

COLON

A colon signals that there will be information listed or given specific to what has just been said.

The Adventures of Tom Sawyer

And now the minister prayed. A good, generous prayer it was, and went into details: it pleaded for the church and the little children of the church; for the other churches of the village; for the village itself; for the county; for the state; for the state officers; for the United States; for the churches of the United States; for Congress; for the President; for the officers of the government; for the poor sailors, tossed by stormy seas; for the oppressed millions groaning under the heel of European monarchies and Oriental despotisms; for such as have the light and good tidings, and yet have not eyes to see nor ears to hear withal; for the heathen in the far islands of the sea; and closed with a supplication that the words he was about to speak might find grace and favor, and be as seed sown in fertile ground, yielding in time a grateful harvest of good. Amen.

Look at the examples of proper punctuation in this excerpt:

○ A colon signals the listing of items the minister prayed for.
○ Capital letters are used at the beginnings of sentences and for proper nouns.
○ Commas are used to signal pauses between adjectives that modify the same noun and between clauses joined by conjunctions.
○ Semicolons are used as signals between the items listed, because many items are lengthy and some include words separated by commas. (Read the passage as if all the semicolons were commas. Confusing, huh?)

ELLIPSIS POINTS

Ellipsis points are three periods, or dots, one following the other. They signal that something has been left out of quoted material.

Sometimes when quoting a sentence, only the beginning and end are wanted. Can you just leave out the middle? No. Quotations must match the original. Use ellipsis points to show that something belongs where the dots are. If the part you want to leave out is at the end of a sentence, use a period followed by the three dots. This will make four dots altogether.

How the British Use Quote Marks

If you were to pick up your own copy of *Alice in Wonderland*, you might notice that the quote marks are different. Instead of using double quotes to mark dialogue, the English often use single quote marks. So, what if someone is quoting something within a quote? That quote is set off with double quotes. (Exactly the opposite of what is done in the United States!)

QUOTATION MARKS

Quotation marks signal one of the following:

1. Someone is speaking.
2. A song, poem, or article is being named.
3. A word is being used in a special way.
4. Someone else's words are being quoted.

Through the Looking Glass

"She can't do Addition," the Red Queen interrupted. "Can you do Subtraction? Take nine from eight."

"Nine from eight I can't, you know," Alice replied very readily: "but—"

"She can't do Subtraction," said the White Queen. "Can you do Division? Divide a loaf by a knife—what's the answer to that?"

Notice the use of quotation marks to signal the beginning and ending of each character's remarks.

Rules to Remember ✔

Do use quotation marks for direct quotations. **Do not** use quotation marks when what people say is reported indirectly. The conversation to the left could be written: The Queen said that Alice couldn't do addition. She asked whether Alice could do subtraction. She interrupted Alice's reply and said Alice couldn't do subtraction either.

Here is a helpful chart to refer to when needed.

PUNCTUATION OF SENTENCE TYPES

1. A period is used at the end of a declarative sentence.

2. A question mark is used at the end of an interrogative sentence.

3. An exclamation point is used at the end of an exclamatory sentence.

4. Either a period or an exclamation point can be used at the end of an imperative sentence. If the order is given abruptly, an exclamation point is more effective. Tip: You can't tell whether a sentence is imperative or exclamatory just by looking for an exclamation point. You can also tell by the message. An exclamatory sentence expresses some kind of feeling. An imperative sentence requests or commands someone to do something. An imperative sentence usually starts with a verb and has an understood subject (you).

5. If a negative sentence asks a question, a question mark is used at the end: Why didn't you tell me? If a negative sentence states that something did not happen or is not so, a period is used: You didn't know the answer.

APOSTROPHE

1. An apostrophe shows possession or ownership.

When the noun is singular, the apostrophe comes between the noun and the *s*. For example: the cat's neck. When the noun is plural, the apostrophe comes after the plural. For example: the robbers' voices.

Plurals are sometimes made by an internal change, such as when *man* changes to *men*. In that case, place the apostrophe as you would for a singular noun. For example: The man's hat/The men's hats.

2. An apostrophe shows the omission of letters in contractions. For example: what's (what is), wouldn't (would not), shouldn't (should not), that's (that is).

3. An apostrophe is used when referring to certain letters or words. For example: There are two p's in <u>apostrophe</u>.

   Apostrophes are used in the same way to talk about words. For example: There are too many <u>and</u>'s in that sentence.

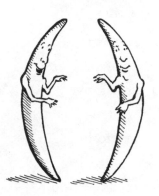

PARENTHESES

Parentheses signal that material is being added that doesn't belong within the structure of the sentence. While the information supplied within the parentheses is needed by the reader immediately, it is inserted with parentheses to show that it is not part of the sentence.

The Adventures of Tom Sawyer

"Tom's younger brother (or rather half brother), Sid . . . was a quiet boy, and had no adventurous, troublesome ways."

● ●

Practice Makes Perfect!

PUNCTUATION LIGHTNING BOLT

You can play this challenging game with just one friend or with a large group.

WHAT YOU NEED: a pencil, paper.

WHAT YOU DO: Each player takes turns trying to get the opposing side to be hit with the lightning bolt—the mark of a mistake!

To take a turn, **say a sentence** out loud. The opposing side must immediately shout out the punctuation used to end it. (Be as creative in your delivery as you like—just remember that whoever's listening will be guessing the kind of sentence from the way you say it!)

Choose from the following: period, exclamation point, question mark, quotation marks (by quoting someone within a sentence), or a combination. For example: You don't mean that. (*period*) Do you? (*question mark*) Why, Mary, I'm shocked! (*exclamation point*) "I just followed the rabbit," she said. (*quotation marks*) **Keep going with a string of sentences.** Then when you stop, the opposing side has to remember them all in order to get the punctuation right! If the wrong punctuation is given, **you can shout** out: "Lightning bolt!" A hit!

3 FORMAL VERSUS INFORMAL ENGLISH AND IDIOMS

Did you know that we have *two* forms of English to use in this country? That's right, and they're called formal and informal English. When you speak to your friends using informal English, you are the boss. You might choose to use expressions called idioms to "color" your conversation. You can even decide whether your listeners will understand what you say.

But when formal English is required, the rules of grammar must be followed.

Let's take a look at formal versus informal English and those colorful expressions called idioms. Then you'll be ready to learn some common pitfalls of grammar and how to avoid them.

FORMAL VERSUS INFORMAL ENGLISH

Informal English is more relaxed in choice of words and word order than formal English. It's the type of casual, everyday language that you might use with your friends. It not only uses slang—made-up words or words given a meaning other than their usual definition—informal English also uses shortcuts. One example is using contractions, such as *didn't* and *can't* instead of the more formal *did not* and *can not*. Or, they could be shortened words, such as *demo* for *demonstration* or *info* for *information*.

But we sometimes need to communicate in a formal way, with formal English, such as in school, when writing letters, reports, compositions, and stories, or when you give speeches. When formal English is required, the rules of grammar are the boss, and the rules about words and word order must be followed.

Why can't we all just speak and write the way we want to, without all the rules? Grammar is a way of organizing communication so that it can be understood by everyone, not just those in a particular group. If we didn't have grammar rules, and only used informal English, it wouldn't be too long before everyone would be speaking their own language, and we couldn't understand each other at all!

Here is an example of the difference between formal and informal English based on word choices. Notice how the same thing can be said in formal and informal English.

FORMAL: "Excuse me, madam, I believe that you called my pedigreed canine companion a mongrel. Please apologize, or I shall have your employment terminated."

INFORMAL: "Hey, lady. Can't you see that this isn't a mutt? You better take that back, or I'll get you fired!"

This example shows the difference between informal and formal English based on word order:

FORMAL: To whom did you give the book?

INFORMAL: Which one did you give the book to?

Now you try. Sometimes the formal English can be even funnier than the informal—mostly because we aren't used to it anymore!

● ●

Practice Makes Perfect!

BATTLE OF THE BANDS

Here's a funny game you can play with your favorite music and at least one other player.

WHAT YOU NEED: a few favorite songs, paper, pencil.

WHAT YOU DO: Many songs are written in informal English (the casual language used with friends). You are going to change some song lyrics to formal English, a more "proper" manner of speaking and writing. First **copy the lyrics of a favorite song** along the left side of a piece of paper. On the right side, **rewrite the lyrics** in a formal manner. (For instance: "I need me some pop for drinkin'" can change to "I require liquid refreshment.") Then **share your rewritten lyrics** with a friend and see if she or he can guess the real lyrics!

• •

IDIOMS

Idioms do not have literal meanings. For a literal meaning, the words mean exactly what they say. But an idiom or idiomatic expression is like a painting done with words. The meaning of the idiom often has little to do with the actual meaning of the words.

Take a look at the following story and see how many idioms you can figure out by reading the story. Check your results with the idioms and their meanings listed on pages 66 through 68.

SAY WHAT?

I went to the museum with my mother. I invited Robert to go with us, but at the last minute he canceled without reason.

"What goes around comes around. There are lots of fish in the sea," my mom said.

Say what? I thought.

We ran into Caroline and her dad in the gift shop. Caroline was flying around, her pigtails flapping.

"Like a bull in a china shop," my mom whispered to me.

What? I thought.

The four of us headed over to the museum cafeteria and stood in the lunch line. I wanted to order a coke, french fries, a bag of potato chips, an ice-cream cone, and a box of mints.

"Whoa. I think your eyes are bigger than your stomach!" my mom exclaimed.

Say what? I thought.

Caroline ordered twice as much as I did. But after I had eaten, I felt sick. She said, "Hah, that's because you always eat too much."

"Oh, yeah?" I replied. "Tell me everything *you* ate yesterday."

My mom said, "Let's not open that can of worms, please."

Now take a look at the meanings of the idioms used in the story. How many did you guess right?

What goes around comes around: However a person treats others will come back to him or her—the same way that something spinning around in a circle eventually reaches its starting point.

There are lots of fish in the sea: Don't worry if you lose a chance at being with someone, because there are many others for you.

Like a bull in a china shop: Someone who tends to break things because they are careless, or someone who tramples over people's feelings without thinking.

Your eyes are bigger than your stomach: You overestimate how much you can eat—or do.

Open a can of worms: The topic (can) brought up for discussion (once opened) might contain some unpleasant things (worms).

Now here are some for you to try! Try writing your own original story using some of these idioms.

See everything as black or white: A person believes everything is either right or wrong, one way or another, with no possibility there might be *some* truth to both sides.

Two left feet: A person is clumsy, as if he or she has two left feet instead of a right and a left.

Trial by fire: You never know how well you will do in a given situation until you face it.

Speak with a forked tongue: (A snake has a forked tongue, and snakes are not trusted.) By someone's manner of speaking, they might not be trusted.

Feel like dancing a jig: (A jig is a dance often done at celebrations.) A person feels happy and joyful.

Off the top of one's head: A person gives an answer without too much thought.

That was one hard nut to crack: (A hard nut is difficult to crack open.) A problem was hard to solve.

Has thick skin: A person is not sensitive to the comments of others.

Saw stars: (People about to lose consciousness sometimes see stars.) A person received a bonk on the head.

Butter wouldn't melt in her mouth: She is not as nice or sweet as she pretends to be.

Two-faced: A person acts falsely and betrays other people's trust (as though he or she had two faces and could then show one face to one person and the other to someone else).

Green-eyed monster: (The color green is often associated with envy and jealousy.) A person who is known for exhibiting jealousy.

More than one string to his bow: (A violin bow has many strings.) A person has many talents.

As broad as it's long: Whichever way you look at an issue, it will look the same, just as something can measure the same in length and width.

● ●

Practice Makes Perfect!

THE DRAMATIC AND INSTAMATIC
PHOTO IDIOM ESSAY

This clever, fun activity uses an instant camera and is perfect for a sleepover, birthday party, or any other event!

WHAT YOU NEED: an instant camera, film, marking pen.

WHAT YOU DO: Think of a few idioms that would look funny in a photograph. **Act each one** out and **take a picture.** You can either label the photos you take or have people guess what the idioms are.

If you run out of film, use the idioms in a game of charades.

Some idioms you can try are *egg on your face, make your hair stand on end, eat your words, on the nose, walking on eggshells, a miss is as good as a mile, a stitch in time saves nine, look before you leap, don't put the cart before the horse,* and *a tin ear.*

● ●

4 COMMON ERRORS

Let's take a look at some common errors in grammar. When you play darts, you want to hit the center of the bull's-eye, and when you communicate, you want your words to hit "dead center," too—that way your listener (or reader) will be sure to get your meaning. Avoiding these errors will help your sentences be on center every time. The following are errors, whether the English you use is formal or informal.

VERB ERRORS

1. CONFUSING THE PAST TENSE AND PAST PARTICIPLE OF VERBS

The past participle uses *has, have,* or *had.* Here are some examples:

Don't say: I could have <u>beat</u> him.
Say: I could have <u>beaten</u> him.

Don't say: She has <u>became</u> my friend.
Say: She has <u>become</u> my friend.

Don't say: I should have <u>began</u> that sooner.
Say: I should have <u>begun</u> that sooner.

Don't say: He could have <u>drove</u> there himself.
Say: He could have <u>driven</u> there himself.

There is a chart of irregular verbs on pages 23 through 25. Practice using these verbs in sentences, for instance: I <u>begin</u>. I <u>am beginning</u>. I <u>began</u>. I <u>have begun</u>. The chart will help you find the correct words to use in your sentences.

2. MIXING UP THE SUBJECT-VERB AGREEMENT

If the subject is singular, the verb is singular. If the subject is plural, the verb must be plural. When two different things are the subject, the subject is plural.

Charles and his dog is going with the boys. (*Is* should be *are* to match the two subjects: *Charles* and *his dog.*)

Our friends said they was going to meet us at the playground. (*Was* should be *were* to match the plural subject: *friends.*)

Grammar Challenge!

Can you find the two verb errors in the sentence below?

He was laying on the ground when he should of been running.

The first error is a past tense error, which comes from incorrect use of the verbs *lie* and *lay*: People *lie* down. They do not *lay* down. *Lay* means to put things down.

The second error is the use of a preposition instead of a helping verb to make the past participle. This error happens because people confuse *of* for *'ve*, the contraction for *have*, as in "he should've been."

PRONOUN ERRORS

1. CONFUSION OF THE OWNERSHIP PRONOUN *THEIR* AND THE ADVERB *THERE*

Use *their* when you want to convey ownership of something and *there* when you want to convey location: I took a chunk out of their apple and threw it over there.

2. CONFUSING CONTRACTIONS AND POSSESSIVE PRONOUNS

Listed on the next page are a few pronouns that are easily confused because they sound exactly the same.

contractions	possessive pronouns
you're	your
there's	theirs
it's	its
who's	whose

Hint: One way to decide whether to use a contraction or a possessive pronoun is to try to break the contraction into its two parts. Take a look:

Their fur coats kept them warm during the Alaskan winter.

Now test it. Do you want to say, "They are fur coats?" No! Then *Their* is correct, not *They're*.

3. A PRONOUN SEPARATED TOO FAR FROM ITS REFERENT (WHAT IT REFERS TO)

For example: The boys were camping beside a fire and swimming in the river and putting more wood on it to warm up.

Did they put wood on the river? No! Rewrite the sentence this way:

The boys were camping beside a fire and put more wood on it to warm up after swimming in the river.

Watch Out for These Pronoun Pitfalls!

Don't say:	**Say:**
He said so hisself.	He said so himself.
They wanted to do all the work theirself.	They wanted to do all the work themselves.
They asked John and myself to be there.	They asked John and me to be there.
Each boy must buy their own notebooks.	Each boy must buy his own notebook.
Just between you and I, she is wrong.	Just between you and me, she is wrong.

Sentence Errors

1. RUN-ON SENTENCE

A run-on sentence has two or more independent clauses that are either joined without using a conjunction or punctuation, or have too many clauses joined by conjunctions. In each case, the sentence should be made into more than one sentence rather than running on. Below you'll find a run-on sentence that should have a semicolon between the clauses, or which should be written as two sentences.

Buck learned from the other sled dogs how to keep warm in the snow they dug little caves in which to bury themselves.

You can put either a semicolon or a period after *snow*. (If you use a period, don't forget to capitalize the first word in the next sentence, *they*.)

Another kind of run-on sentence overuses the conjunction *and* to join clause after clause:

Huck and Tom were in an abandoned house and they were looking for hidden treasure and they heard two robbers coming in and they hid in the attic and they were scared to death and they heard the robbers searching and the robbers found the treasure.

Imagine reading this aloud. You would have to stop to take a breath!

2. SENTENCE FRAGMENT

A sentence fragment is either a dependent clause or a group of words without a subject and a predicate.

Waiting at the corner in the cold for half an hour. This fragment does not tell a complete thought. It has no subject. A sentence must have both a subject and a predicate:

Tom waited at the corner in the cold for half an hour.

3. DANGLING MODIFIER

A modifier describes something. To avoid misunderstanding, it needs to be with the thing it modifies, or describes. So don't leave a poor modifier dangling where it doesn't belong!

They put the money in the bank they found in the middle of the road.

Did they find the *bank* in the middle of the road? No! Rewrite the sentence to read: They put the money they found in the middle of the road in the bank.

• •

Practice Makes Perfect!
THE GRAMMAR ERRORS POSTER

Be on the lookout for bad grammar dudes by creating this poster to keep on a wall in your room. The poster will display those mean, ugly, and desperate bad dudes known as common errors!

WHAT YOU NEED: a large sheet of poster paper, markers, pen, pencil, ungrammatical sentences (found in newspapers, local papers, and advertisements, or in your own writing).

WHAT YOU DO: At the top of your sheet of poster paper, **write "MOST WANTED."** Underneath, **write "Put Errors Where They Belong!"** Then, using the illustration as a guide, **draw several bars** running about two-thirds down the page. Allow enough room between the bars to "jail" your ungrammatical sentences. In the space below, **correct the sentences**. If you want, you can write the correct sentences inside large keys. Be creative—draw a few bad guys lurking behind the bars.

You don't have to fill in every bar right away. Choose only those errors you have problems with to help you remember what's correct.

Here are some ideas to get you started:

Jack and myself went together. (reflexive pronoun used instead of subjective or objective pronoun)

We was just coming for you. (pronoun-verb disagreement)

Those kind of cookies are my favorite. (pronoun-noun-verb disagreement)

Their on they're way. (pronoun-contraction confusion)

You should of came. I should have went. (verb tense error and preposition *of* instead of *have*)

5 VOCABULARY AND SPELLING

Words! You need them to communicate, and you need to be able to spell them correctly to communicate effectively. Otherwise, you could find yourself eating a wooden stake and a sandy desert for dinner, instead of a sizzling steak and creamy dessert! Read on to find tips on choosing the right words for what you want to say, as well as helpful spelling lists.

HOMONYMS

Homonyms are words, such as *steak* and *stake,* that sound the same but are not spelled the same and do not have the same meaning.

Out loud, read this conversation between the Red Queen and Alice to see how homonyms can confuse.

Through the Looking Glass

"Can you answer useful questions?" she said. "How is bread made?"
"I know that!" Alice cried eagerly. "You take some flour—"
"Where do you pick the flower?" the White Queen asked.
"In a garden or in the hedges?"
"Well, it isn't picked at all," Alice explained. "It's ground—"
"How many acres of ground?" said the White Queen. "You mustn't leave out so many things."

You probably noticed that two of the words that caused confusion were not spelled the same though they sounded the same! These words, *flour* and *flower,* are homonyms.

You also probably noticed some confusion over the word *ground.* These two *grounds* are not homonyms, they are homographs. Homographs are spelled the same but have different meanings. Sometimes homographs are pronounced the same and sometimes they are pronounced differently. You don't have to worry about mixing up their spelling, but you do need to pay attention to their pronunciation.

Here are some examples of homographs:

a fish, bass (pronounced "bass") versus a low tone, bass (pronounced "base") a boat front, bow (pronounced "bow") and to bend over, bow (also pronounced "bow") versus an arrow shooter, bow (pronounced "boh") and a ribbon, bow (also pronounced "boh")

Here are some examples of how homonyms might cause spelling errors:

You look *pail,* are you feeling okay? (pale)
I ripped it; can you *so* it? (sew)
There is only one *write* way to do it. (right)
It is too strong to break; it's made from *steal.* (steel)
It is down in the *seller* with the rest of the junk. (cellar)
It's just *to* hard to get slippers on a cat. (too)
"Give *piece* a chance" is my favorite John Lennon lyric. (peace)
It's easy for you to say, but I just don't have *patients* for this thing. (patience)
The *mane* thing is just to try to get it on straight. (main)
I'll give you my *pare* of sunglasses for your CD. (pair)

Cartoonists are always on the lookout for homonyms, because their confusion can make you laugh. For example: " My goodness! Did you say that diamond was worth 24 carrots?"

Practice Makes Perfect!

HILARIOUS HOMONYMS

Try your hand at becoming a cartoonist using homonyms.

WHAT YOU NEED: a pencil, paper, a ruler, colored pencils, pen.

WHAT YOU DO: Jokes and funny situations are often based upon confusing one homonym for another. **Come up with some homonyms** you think you can use to make a joke. **Look at cartoons** in the newspaper. Notice how each cartoon is drawn in a "strip," or a series of boxes. Each box leads toward the punchline. With your homonyms, **plan out your joke** over a series of scenes. Figure out how many boxes you'll need. **Draw your cartoon lightly** in pencil, including the words in speech balloons. Once it is finished, **ink it over** with a pen. Then **color it in** using colored pencils.

Easy-to-Confuse Words
(and how to un-confuse them!)

1. WORDS THAT LOOK OR SOUND SIMILAR

Some words that are not homonyms or homographs cause confusion anyway because they look or sound so similar. Here are some:

Well, my little *angle,* come to mama. (angel)
Hand over your *desert,* I'm starving. (dessert)
Well, sir, that was disgusting, downright *vial.* (vile)
Don't just *except* defeat. (accept)
Do we all have *are* things? (our)
I can't eat *diary,* I am allergic to milk. (dairy)

2. SOUNDING OUT WORDS INCORRECTLY

Pronounce a word right and you'll have a better chance of spelling it right! "Height" not "heighth," "mischievous" not "mischievious." Of course, with some words it's downright hard to tell the spelling by the pronunciation—for example, *habitat* not *habetat* or *habatat*; *habitual* not *habichual*; *gruel* not *grool*; *gorilla* not *gurilla.*

Foolproof Spelling!

Not sure how to spell a word? Look it up in the dictionary!

DON'T LEAVE MY "L" OUT! IT HAS A RIGHT TO BE SEEN, TOO!

3. OMITTED SILENT LETTERS

Sometimes letters are dropped because they are silent. Since you might not know the "shy" little letters are there, you might leave them out when you spell them! For instance, along with the *p* in raspberry and the *l* in salmon, don't leave out the *d* in handsome—your prince might get annoyed!

4. COMPOUND WORDS VERSUS HYPHENATED COMPOUNDS

Sometimes when two words combine to make one, they have two of the same letters where they join. What should you do? Drop one of them? Better to keep them both, as in *glowworm, bookkeeping, overrated, overrun, overrule,* and *drunkenness.*

Just don't join three of the same letters together, as in *stilllife.* That's what hyphenated compound words are for! Hyphenated compound words are two words that are joined together with a hyphen to show they are joined but not blended, such as *good-natured* or *soft-spoken.*

How do you know when to hyphenate and when not to? First, think of words as dating, and you will get used to seeing them together. Second, they get engaged, and a hyphen (like a ring) joins them. Third, they are married and become blended. Here are some blended words: *Overjoyed, overhear, notebook, noteworthy, mouthpiece, offshoot, oilcloth, onlooker, overcome, overweight, overwork, overhaul, pickpocket, pincushion, playground, praiseworthy,* and *hateful.*

Here are some words that are still in the hyphenated (engaged) stage: *one-way, stiff-necked, fast-moving.*

Rules to Remember

Use hyphens for number pairs (twenty-one) or for fractions between the numerator and denominator (four-fifths). Do not divide reflexive pronouns with a hyphen: *myself,* not *my-self*; *himself,* not *him-self.*

· ·

Practice Makes Perfect!

THE COMPOUND WORD SCULPTURE

Make a creative art project, using cardboard, to build a sculpture of related compound words.

WHAT YOU NEED: lightweight cardboard, marking pen, scissors, toothpicks, tape, clay, shoebox lid.

WHAT YOU DO: Start with a compound word and add other related compound words that can be built into a word sculpture. For example: *silversmith → silverware → cookware → cookbook → bookworm → earthworm → earthquake → earthenware → warehouse → playhouse → houseclean → cleanup → holdup → household → playhouse*. You may want to use a dictionary to help you. **Cut out several square strips** from the lightweight poster board and **write a word** on each strip. **Connect the word strips** together with toothpicks and tape to make a sculpture. The only rule is that the words you connect must have one word in common, such as *silversmith* and *silverware*.

You **may want to attach your sculpture** to the shoebox lid, using clay to hold it in place.

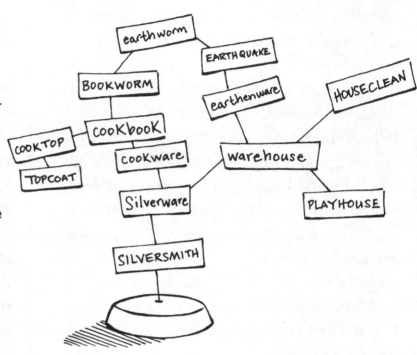

● ●

5. CONFUSION WITH *IM/IMM* AND *IN/INN* PREFIXES

These prefixes often cause trouble and are misspelled or misused because you need to know when to double the *m* or *n*. Look at these examples:

imbecile, imitate, imagine; immeasurable, immature, immune, immediate, immaculate, immigrate, immovable, imminent, immemorial, immense;

inconceivable, inconsiderate, inaccessible, inaccurate, inconspicuous, inappropriate, inoculate; innocent, innovate, innumerable.

6. MIXING UP WORD PATTERNS

Word patterns are made by letter combinations. An example would be *ou, ough,* and *ow.* Learn to identify a word pattern based upon its sounds as well as its spellings. You'll find examples of the following word patterns on pages 83 through 87:

- ❍ *tion* words
- ❍ *ei* and *ie* words
- ❍ *ee* and *ea* words
- ❍ *mm* words
- ❍ *ble, able, ible, dle, gle,* and *el* words
- ❍ *oo, ou,* and *ow* words
- ❍ *er* and *or* words

SPELLING WORDS AND LISTS

The following word lists and spelling lists will start you on your way to good spelling. They won't list all the words you'll ever need—if they did, you wouldn't be able to lift this book! But they will show you how to recognize word groups and word patterns. The lists include:

- ❍ compound and hyphenated words
- ❍ silent letter words
- ❍ pattern words
- ❍ 240 common spelling words
- ❍ homographs and homonyms

All spelling words and word lists were chosen from the extensive fourth, fifth, and sixth grade word lists given in Children's Writer's Word Book, Alijandra Mogilner, Ph.D., Writer's Digest Books, F&W Publications, Cincinnati, 1992.

COMPOUND AND HYPHENATED WORDS

airtight	blackmail	blacksmith	bloodshed
bloodthirsty	bodyguard	boyfriend	boyhood
breakwater	bridesmaid	broadcast	broadcloth
brownstone	buckskin	bumblebee	buttonhole
careless	caretaker	carload	clambake
clergyman	commonwealth	cornmeal	cowboy
downhearted	earthenware	earthquake	elsewhere
evergreen	eyeglasses	fingernail	fingerprint
firecracker	flagpole	folklore	forecast
forefather	forehead	foreman	foresight
freshwater	girlfriend	goldenrod	goldfinch
good-natured	gooseberry	grapefruit	guidepost
half-mast	hillside	homespun	hindquarter
hothouse	landslide	lightweight	loincloth
lowland	mainland	milestone	mock-up
moonbeam	moonlight	oarlock	oatmeal
outrage	outright	outward	outwit
overflow	overlook	overseas	overtake
overwhelm	peppermint	pineapple	pipeline
radioactive	redwood	saber-toothed	sagebrush
salesperson	shipwreck	showroom	skyline
stovepipe	tablecloth	tablespoon	three-fourths
tiptoe	toenail	underground	viewpoint
warehouse	wasteland	widespread	

Silent Letter Words

comb (kohm)   Buddhist (bood-ist)   debris (de-bree)   column (kol-um)

knave (nave)   subtle (sut-ul)   thumb (thum)

Pattern Words

tion

affection	ambition	ammunition	association
aviation	caption	caution	combustion
compensation	competition	congregation	conscription
constellation	consternation	convention	conversation
corporation	delegation	destruction	elevation
emotion	evolution	expedition	flotation
formation	foundation	fraction	friction
function	generation	information	inscription
intention	justification	mention	nutrition
occupation	partition	plantation	portion
production	promotion	proportion	protection
reception	recreation	registration	relation
reputation	requisition	resolution	respiration
revolution	salvation	sanction	sedition
sensation	situation	solution	superstition
temptation	tradition		

ei

ceiling	conceited	conceive	deceive
deity	foreign	forfeit	height

PATTERN WORDS (CONTINUED)

ei (continued)

heir	leisure	perceive	receipt
reign	sovereign	vein	

ie

achieve	alien	conscience	convenient
fiery	fried	frontier	handkerchief
patient	piecemeal	pier	pierce
relief	relieve	retrieve	review
shield	shriek	siege	sieve
yield			

ee

creed	flee	leek	levee
privateer	redeem	screech	sheer
sneer	sweep	weep	

ea

cleat	crease	defeat	eager
flea	grease	hearth	hearty
heave	leak	lease	mead
mean	meatloaf	peak	pear
pearl	peasant	preach	release
research	seam	sergeant	shear
swear	veal	weary	wreath

mm

accommodate	comment	commentary	commerce
commission	committee	commodity	commonwealth
commotion	communion	glimmer	grammar
immaculate	immature	immigration	immobile
shimmer			

ble, able, ible

amble	assemble	Bible	bumble
capable	credible	fable	feeble
formidable	fumble	gamble	gobble
grumble	habitable	humble	incredible
invisible	liable	marble	miserable
mumble	nibble	notable	pebble
sable	scramble	sensible	stable
stumble	syllable	treble	tumble
visible	wobble		

dle

bundle	cuddle	fiddle	girdle
idle	kindle	ladle	poodle
saddle	waddlc		

gle

dangle	gargle	goggle	jungle
mingle			

PATTERN WORDS *(CONTINUED)*

el

angel	barrel	channel	cruel
propel	sentinel	snorkel	towel

oo

bloom	boomerang	boon	booth
brooch	brood	droop	hoop
lagoon	loom	loop	moor
proof	saloon	snooze	vamoose
woo			

ou

aloud	astound	background	bounce
camouflage	couch	counter	countess
courage	courtesy	crouch	devour
dough	encourage	enormous	flounder
flourish	foul	outer	profound
pronounce	recount	roust	shroud
slouch	thorough	tremendous	trousers
trout			

ow

arrowhead	bellow	bestow	brow
burrow	cowardly	fowl	furrow
gallows	gown	growl	howl

| lowland | mellow | minnow | pillow |
| shallow | sorrow | vow | |

er

blister	cancer	canter	gutter
limber	linger	logger	manager
peddler	plumber	plunder	porter
revolver	scamper	shatter	shudder
shutter	simmer	sober	stagger
surrender	swagger	taper	temper
thermometer	timber	utter	

or

| anchor | mirror | professor | sculptor |
| splendor | | | |

240 Common Spelling Words

abbreviate	absence	accessory	accident
according	accuse	accustom	achieve
acknowledge	affection	aggressive	allowance
aloud	angel	anguish	ankle
anticipate	anxiety	apologize	appetite
appreciate	approve	artificial	ashamed
assemble	assertive	assistant	association
astonish	astound	attitude	bargain
barrel	behavior	beverage	brilliant

240 COMMON SPELLING WORDS (CONTINUED)

bruise
cabinet
candidate
canine

capable
capacity
cautious
ceiling

channel
civilization
comedian
commercial

commit
committee
communicate
competition

compliment
conceited
confidential
congratulate

conscience
conspicuous
contagious
convenient

conversation
correspond
courtesy
dangerous

deliberate
depression
design
diamond

difficult
disappoint
discipline
discontinue

disguise
distinguish
duplicate
ecology

embarrass
emotion
emphasize
encounter

encourage
enormous
envelope
environment

essential
eventually
exaggerate
experience

fantastic
fascinate
fatigue
feeble

fiction
fierce
flexible
flourish

foreign
fortunate
fragile
freight

friction
frightened
generous
genius

genuine
gigantic
glimpse
gorgeous

guarantee
guilty
handkerchief
headache

height
hideous
hoarse
horizontal

hostile
identify
illustration
imitate

immature
impatient
impression
inconvenient

incredible
ingredient
intelligent
jealous

jungle
junior
justification
juvenile

kindle
kneel
knuckle
laboratory

ladle	launch	laundry	lawyer
leisure	linger	literature	luggage
magician	magnificent	maintain	mingle
miniature	miracle	mischief	miserable
mosquito	musical	naughty	nourish
nuisance	numerous	obligation	obstacle
obvious	occupation	opponent	organize
paradise	paragraph	particular	passenger
patient	peculiar	penetrate	permanent
personality	photograph	practical	precious
preliminary	principle	privilege	qualify
quantity	quarrel	quote	receipt
recipe	recommend	request	residence
responsible	restaurant	retrieve	review
ridiculous	routine	sacrifice	sample
schedule	scheme	section	sensible
sensitive	serious	signature	significant
similar	situation	slaughter	solution
squeeze	substantial	supervise	suspicion
tedious	television	temperature	temporary
tempt	terrific	thorough	tobacco
tragedy	traitor	treasure	tremendous
triumph	universe	urgent	various
vehicle	version	vicious	virtually
vocabulary	volcano	volunteer	wail
whistle	wreck	wrench	wrestle

HOMOGRAPHS AND HOMONYMS

aid, aide

Aid means "help." *Aide* is an assistant or helper.

ant, aunt

Ant is an insect. *Aunt* is a mother's sister.

ate, eight

Ate is the past tense of *to eat*, which means "to take in food." *Eight* is the number that comes after *seven*.

bare, bear

Bare means "plain, undecorated, or naked." *Bear* is an animal.

blue, blew

Blue is a primary color. *Blue* also means "sad." *Blew* is the past tense of *to blow*, which means "to move air."

ceiling, sealing

Ceiling is the top or roof of a room. *Sealing* is the present participle of *to seal*, which means "to close or fasten."

cell, sell

Cell is a small room, as in a jail. *Sell* means "to part with goods for money."

cent, scent, sent

Cent is a penny coin. *Scent* is an odor, or smell. *Sent* is the past tense of *to send*, which means "to cause something to go somewhere else."

chute, shoot

Chute is a channel for water or other material to move through quickly. *Shoot* means "to pull a trigger or other mechanism in order to hit a target with a missile."

dear, deer

Dear means "something of value." It also means "expensive." *Deer* is an animal.

fair, fare

Fair means "even or equal." *Fair* also means "fair-haired" or "fair-complected." *Fair* is a kind of festival, too. *Fare* is the amount paid to travel by bus, taxi, train, or airplane.

flee, flea

Flee means "to go away quickly," as to escape. *Flea* is an insect.

grate, great

Grate is a metal cover that is placed over a hole in the sidewalk or road or put on a barbecue grill. *Grate* also means "to shred." *Great* means "very good" or "very large."

hall, haul

Hall is a narrow passageway in a building, a small entry room, or a large room for assembling. *Haul* means "to carry or transport items in a cart or truck."

here, hear

Here means "in this place." *Hear* means "to catch sound using the ears."

hole, whole

Hole is a break in the surface of something solid, such as clothing or the ground. *Whole* means "the entire amount, all there is, undivided in any way."

horse, hoarse

Horse is an animal. *Hoarse* is a raspy, grating sound of a voice.

knew, new

Knew is the past tense of *to know,* which means "to be aware of." *New* means "novel" or "not there before." It is the opposite of old.

loan, lone

Loan is something borrowed that must be returned. *To loan* means "to lend." *Lone* means "only one" or "alone."

meat, meet

Meat is the flesh of animals. *Meet* means "to come together."

HOMOGRAPHS AND HOMONYMS (CONTINUED)

medal, meddle

Medal is an award for an achievement. *Meddle* means "to interfere."

night, knight

Night is the part of the day after evening. *Knight* is a person of title in England, or a person who wore armor, rode a horse, and fought for the king in medieval times.

our, hour

Our is a possessive pronoun meaning "belonging to us." *Hour* is a unit of time equal to sixty minutes.

pair, pare, pear

Pair is two things that go together. *Pare* means "to peel." *Pear* is a fruit.

passed, past

Passed is the past tense of *to pass,* which means "to go by" or "to succeed in a test," or "to move up a grade in school." *Past* means "a time before."

pause, paws

Pause means "to wait" or "a short time of waiting." *Paws* are an animal's feet.

principal, principle

Principal is the main person or thing, such as the school principal. *Principle* is the idea or method by which something works.

rain, reign, rein

Rain is drops of water that fall from clouds. *Reign* means "to rule." *Rein* is a strap used to give directions to or to lead a horse.

right, rite, write

Right is a direction or side opposite left. *Right* also means "correct" or "to make correct." *Rite* is a ceremony, such as a christening, marriage, or funeral. *Write* means "to put words on paper or another surface" or "to compose a piece of literature."

route, root

Route is a path or way of getting from place to place. *Root* is the part in the earth that anchors and carries nourishment to a plant. *Root* also means "to dig around looking for something."

scene, seen

Scene is a view of something. *Scene* also is a part of a play. *Seen* is the past participle of *to see,* which means "to detect by sight."

stair, stare

Stair is a step. *Stare* means "to look at something steadily for a long time."

tail, tale

Tail is a part of an animal. *Tail* also means "to follow closely." *Tale* is a story.

their, there, they're

Their is a possessive pronoun meaning "belonging to them." *There* means "in that place." *They're* is a contraction meaning "they are."

to, too, two

To is a preposition used to introduce a phrase. It means "coming in the direction of." *Too* is an adverb meaning "also" or "the degree of some quality," as in *too much, too soon, too many. Two* is the number that comes after one.

wait, weight

Wait is a verb meaning "to spend time in expectation of something." It can also mean "to serve at tables in a restaurant." *Weight* is a measure of how heavy or how light things are.

weather, whether

Weather means "the condition of the atmosphere," such as hot, cold, wet, or dry. *Whether* is a conjunction meaning "if," used to introduce a choice.

whose, who's

Whose is a possessive pronoun meaning "belonging to who(m)." *Who's* is a contraction meaning "who is."

HOMOGRAPHS AND HOMONYMS (CONTINUED)

wood, would

Wood is the material that comes from trees. *Would* is the past tense of the verb *will,* which means "to intend to do in the future."

wring, ring

Wring is a verb meaning "to twist around," as in twisting wet cloth to get rid of the water. *Ring* is a piece of jewelry worn on the finger. *Ring* also means "a circle," or "to circle." *Ring* means "to cause a bell to make a sound," too.

your, you're

Your is a possessive pronoun meaning "belonging to you." *You're* is a contraction meaning "you are."

INDEX